See the World!

Warren Bluhm

warrenbluhm.com

Contents

Introduction

My favorite flower is the echinacea, aka coneflower. My life partner and eventual wife, whom I've called Red in my writings over the years, was a genius at coaxing echinacea out of the soil. Wherever she lived, eventually coneflower blooms were everywhere.

On the day she died in early summer 2023, I came home from the hospice and found the first echinacea flowers of the season, including the perfect bloom just outside our front door that I preserved in the photo on the front cover of this collection. I took it as her way of telling me, "I'm OK, and you're going to be OK," from her new home in eternity.

This book is the tenth collection of musings from my daily blog, and this one is on the subject of paying attention — of seeing what's around us instead of walking through the day in a distracted haze. If I had not been looking and seeing the world around me, I may have missed Red's message.

I have been sharing poems, prose poems, flash fiction, and other odds and ends ever since I discovered what a blog is, about 20 years ago, and every day since Aug. 1, 2020. There is little rhyme or reason to what I share, but I do have a couple of themes.

First, I want what I write to encourage, enlighten, and/or entertain.

Second, I want to reflect what Jesus said were the two greatest laws, on which all of his teaching was based: Love God, and love our neighbors, and by the way everyone on Earth is a neighbor.

I hope and pray that you will find those messages in the words that follow.

Warren Bluhm
May 2025

See the world!

I have a new resolution: See the world.
It's not what you think. I'm not planning to reallocate my resources so I can go explore ruins or exotic islands and rain forests and teeming cities.

No: I aim to *see* the world.

I resolve to look around me and see not just the sleeping dogs and dust bunnies but the way the sun brightens and nourishes everything it touches — and the rain, too, in its turn. I plan to be aware of how the air fills my lungs differently when I consciously take in a breath as opposed to leaving the automatic pilot in control.

I plan to notice the echinacea and the compass plants that have bloomed in recent days, and I intend to watch the bees and the beetles visit the new flowers to do their thing. I plan to watch the pelicans fly high overhead and contemplate what they see from their vantage point.

When I resolve to see the world, I expect to see things that sadden as much as delight me, but I expect most of all to see things that fascinate me, for the world is nothing if not fascinating. See how much there is to see! Perhaps that's why our eyes glaze over and we forget to look: There is just so much, and when we try to see it all, our senses overload. But how much we miss when we pass over and shut it down!

I'm not talking about the sensory overload from doom-scrolling and media shouting and artificial intelligence and algorithms — no, I'm talking about what I see when I lift my eyes from the screen to the hills, to the sky, and to the wonders right next to me, just beyond my reach, whether it's a rabbit frozen in my back yard hoping I don't see it or a weed growing between the cracks in an ancient sidewalk.

See the world! I'm not talking about taking a journey through soul-sapping airports for hours and days to see what there is to see far, far away, although you're certainly welcome to do so. I'm talking about seeing the world where you're planted, being aware of the wonder and the beauty and, yes, the appalling and the ugly, the right here and the right now.

We grow accustomed to our surroundings, to our world, to our quotidian, so much so that we stop seeing it, and in doing so we rob ourselves of life itself. We are meant to see the world — every part of it, every second — and to drink it in, and savor it, and change what we can and accept what we can't, but to see it all.

Look! Taste and see! Isn't it fascinating?

Music in every moment

I was having a spot of trouble pulling the trigger as it came time to finish this book. I had a pile of 67 reflections, plus the introduction, plus the closing Author's Note to plug my other books. The trouble was figuring out in what order to present them. There are literally millions, if not quadrillions, of ways to arrange 67 objects.

I now have the entries arranged roughly by the four seasons, from late December through the following December. The awkward thing is that this is a collection of blog posts from 2021 to 2025, and my darling Red passed away smack in the middle of that time frame. By following month to month, I am mourning Red on one page, and a page or two later I'm describing a moment that Red and I just shared.

Would it work if I arranged them in roughly chronological order? But then it's not arranged thematically anymore.

Should I just say, "Oh, the heck with it, just ship the book and move on to the next one?"

The overarching theme is "see the world!" in the sense of being aware of this world we're walking through, noticing the delightful little details we otherwise might miss as we scurry from here to there.

For example, I write this on a May morning with the window open. A bit of a breeze is rustling the wind chimes, and I hear the calls of red-winged blackbirds and cardinals and other bird calls I should be able to identify but am too lazy to memorize.

I live near a major rural highway that links a tourist paradise to Green Bay and the rest of the world, and so the dull roar of tires speeding along on concrete is a constant backdrop, especially in these days when spring is slowly easing toward summer.

And I just noticed that occasionally the wind is brisk enough today to add the sound of a gust to the wind chimes, bird song and everything else.

That's what I mean when I say "see the world!" although just now I guess I'm encouraging you to "listen to the world!" There's music in every moment, beauty wherever you look.

I suspect the solution to my conundrum is to add this passage to the introduction, or as a 68th reflection early on, publish the book in its current configuration, and move along. Readers can be very forgiving souls if they know the author's intentions.

And as long as I was making last-minute revisions, I added a couple of more after that, to make it an even 70 or, with the intro and author's note, 72 reflections, one for each year of my life so far. How cool is that?

The Journey

We are born. We unfold and grow.
We have seasons of light and dark.
We have seasons of warmth and cold.
We slow. We die.
It happens to all of us.

We are all on the same journey, including those we hate, resent, use, abuse, envy and just don't understand.

Would it not be a better use of our precious time to find ways to love our neighbors?

A Declaration of Peace

W hen, in the course of human events, it becomes necessary to step back and ask, "What in the world are we doing?" and consider a different approach, it behooves us to explain what in the world we are doing, and why.

These truths ought to be self-evident — that all humans are created equal, endowed by our Creator with rights that are certain and unalienable, that among these are life, liberty and the pursuit of happiness — but then governments are created to tinker with those rights, to abridge those rights, and eventually to trample those rights.

Ostensibly governments are created to do those things that individuals cannot do, but there are many acts that individuals will not do and should not do, and they are no less heinous when committed in the name of government, and among these are theft, extortion, blackmail, and murder.

As a free and independent human, therefore, I declare that I am at peace with my fellow humans and that I will not initiate violence against them. This I pledge by my life, my fortune (such as it is) and my sacred honor, so help me God.

So help me God

As I was composing my little "Declaration of Peace," I found myself wondering how I could possibly fulfill such a pledge — to never initiate force and to approach everyone in a spirit of "Love My Neighbor" — until I got to the last four words: so help me God.

We have an innate understanding that this universe is in the hands of something bigger than us, and we spend our lives seeking that someone, often in all the wrong places, such as in the form of other humans.

Governments try to assume that "bigger than us" role, but they cannot, no matter how much they cajole and threaten and worse, because in the end they are comprised of other fallible humans, after all.

They cannot take the place of the authentic Higher Power, who instructed us to Love God and Love Our Neighbors and even to love our enemies. When we get right down to it, we are simply incapable of such a love within our own meager means. In need of assistance, we ask, "so, help me, God."

As the apostle Paul wrote to the people of Philippi, I can indeed fulfill my declaration of peace, or love my enemies, because I can do all things with the help of Christ, who strengthens me.

The world through
new eyes

"Stuff your eyes with wonder," Mr. Bradbury said. "Live as if you'd drop dead in 10 seconds. See the world. It's more fantastic than any dream made or paid for in factories."

What a way to see the world. I wrote that quote in my journal a few weeks ago, and it turned into my resolution to "see the world."

"Stuff your eyes with wonder." Do you ever stop in wonder about what a remarkable device an eye is? You might, if you shut your eyes tight and try walking around the room. Don't peek! Now open them and consider how these two little orbs, wired to your brain, take the world and transform it into something you can understand — the colors, the obstacles in your path, the people and flora and fauna around you, the words!

Turn your head in any direction, and there is so much to see. Your eyes are stuffed with imagery! How can you contemplate what's right in front of you and not be filled with wonder?

When we wake up in the morning, no one is promised they will see the sunset. Might you drop dead in 10 seconds? Could this be the day you breathe your last? It's always within the realm of possibility. You're not completely certain a heart attack or brain aneurysm won't snatch your body away from you a few seconds from

now, or a runaway semi truck won't crumple your car beyond recog-
nition, or a meteor won't land on your house.

How do you live as if you'd drop dead in 10 seconds? See the
world! Love your neighbor! Hug your family and your friends and
your puppies! (Cats may be hugged, too, if they will let you.) Pay
attention!

I am as guilty as anyone of neglecting the wonder in every
corner of my life. My eyes glaze over as I drive past vistas as breath-
taking as any on Earth. I doomscroll until I have lost more than a
few precious minutes. I tut-tut over what some idiotic politician has
said or done, and I wonder what has become of the world.

But then I open my journal, and my eyes happen to land on Mr.
Bradbury's encouragement, and I look about the room and out the
window, and I see the world, the marvelous, miraculous world that is
still there and beckoning us to use your life to be alive! And my eyes
and ears fill up with all there is to see, and I'm so glad I thought to
write down those words.

This, this, I suspect, is why I wrote them down in the first place.

Still me

I know my back aches more than it used to. That left knee is really starting to be a distraction. I know sometimes I pause mid-sentence in frustration, because I just can't think of the right word and I know the word has come to my mind dozens if not hundreds of times before. I know I have to stop and sit more often when I am walking or doing physical work — and speaking of walking, I know I'd rather not run anymore, even if I'm in a hurry.

And yet I'm looking out at the world with the same consciousness that looked out at the world to find Spider-Man #4 in a pile of other comic books for sale in the summer of 1963. These are the same fingers and arms that held a woman for the first time in the 1970s with all the wonder and delight that can mean. I am still the young man who watched, fascinated, as stupid people hurled eggs at a stage in Oshkosh because they didn't like what Mr. Reagan was saying about freedom and tyranny.

Of course my opinions and frame of mind have changed in all these years, but it's still me.

I look in the mirror and see the same person who looked in the mirror and saw an underweight tall drink of water, even though now I see an overweight old man with a beer belly.

All I'm trying to say is that the externals have changed and quite a few points of view have changed — although I still believe Reagan was right when he said government IS the problem — but the consciousness that powers these fingers across the page and sees and hears the world around it is still the same consciousness, even if it doesn't see or hear as clearly as it did back in olden times.

We only get one body and one consciousness in this lifetime, and we're stuck with them for a very long time, so it's best we take care of them and feed them right and use them with as much wisdom as we can muster.

It is time

The turning of the year always seems to bring out introspection in people. Wednesday morning, Dec. 29, 2021, I found myself going back over some of the same old thoughts and propping myself up with the same old motivations with a, shall we say, a new resolve? RESOLVE, noun, with the same root as "resolution." Ah yes, the same old same old, but I really mean it this time, Mom! We shall see.

I am, living as I do near the shores of the bay of Green Bay, a Packers fan. As the fourth quarter of Super Bowl XLV began, the Green and Gold led 21-17 but the Pittsburgh Steelers were moving upfield toward a potential go-ahead touchdown. In a moment famously captured by a camera person, defensive coach Kevin Greene grabbed hold of talented Clay Matthews, looked him in the eye and said, "It is time. It is TIME. IT IS TIME."

On the first play of the fourth quarter, Matthews barreled into the ball carrier and knocked the ball loose. The Packers recovered the fumble, scored another touchdown a few plays later, and eventually won the game 31-26.

So: Am I going to react to the motivation like Clay Matthews, get the ball and win the Super Bowl? That sounds much more fun than running out the clock and hoping for the best. What's it going to be? "Prevent defense" or a go-after-the-ball blitz?

I think I want the ball. I still get a little thrill when I think about sitting down and manipulating words until I have something grand or lovely or exciting or all of the above.

What's making me hesitate is all those years of having that feeling and, instead, sputtering and letting it drop and chitty chitty bang bang oh man it stalled out again ...

I'm into the fourth quarter and it's a tie so far, or perhaps a slight lead. I've made a touchdown or two, maybe a field goal, but the end is not far away and the W is not quite nailed down.

IT IS TIME. Oh, yeah, I've written some books, even sold a few handfuls, I've blogged more than 500 straight days, picked up some followers, got a couple dozen email readers whom I rarely regale.

IT IS TIME. What is it I want to say? I always say my objective is to "Entertain – Enlighten – Encourage." Meh. My mission statement/vision consists of three wandering generalities. Let's be more specific.

I want to encourage people to use their brains and common sense and take initiatives. Encourage people to act with fearless freedom and not let busybodies and bullies run their lives.

I want to enlighten people about what came before – fun but semi-forgotten books and songs and TV and radio, and thoughts like Wallace D. Wattles' "you are a creator, not a competitor."

("Not a competitor"? Then what's with the football analogy? Well, it's an analogy not because it's an exact fit but because the example is similar. We ARE competitors but not against each other. We're playing a game, fighting to the death against Father Time, and winning is not defined as beating him but by playing the best game we can in the allotted four quarters, however long they last. And what is the best game? "Love the Lord your God and Love Your Neighbor." And we are all neighbors. Right, Mr. Rogers?)

I want to entertain and give the world adventures, stories that do all of the above and a few thrills and chills and spills — but after every chill a warming, after every spill an ascent.

Those thoughts are a little more focused, and here I sit a half-hour after starting to write, a little hesitant, a little inspired, and not sure what to do next.

"Just get started." Who said that?

It is time.

Feel the breeze your speed generates

Find your pulse.

What makes your heart beat stronger?

Take it by the hand and run – run as fast and as far as your dreams will take you.

Learn how to be who your fancy imagines.

Choose whimsy.

It is good to know where you're going; it is better to enjoy the run.

Feel the breeze in your face that's generated by your speed –

Find your pulse – find what makes your heart beat strong.

Follow that dream. Run it down. Quick as you can!

Joy and contentment wait there, and yes, sometimes frustration and disappointment, but still tempered by the knowledge that you ran as fast and as far as your dreams would take you.

And when it's time to stop running, you'll be able to say that you passed this way and that, and that you chased your dream, if not every step of the way, then as far as you could.

And it was good.

So may we start

This was my blog post for Jan. 1, 2025.

And here we are, 366 days later. Another First of January. Another blank slate.

Last year in this space, I wrote a piece called "Preface" that was intentionally intended to be the preface of a book that became *A Declaration of Peace*. This year I am not as clear about how to start.

The beginning of the year lends itself to new beginnings, and new beginnings are wonderful and hopeful and exciting and joyful. But continuing is also important.

I started a thread last Jan. 1 that became a book about how war is a crime and that we should be declaring peace to one another, not declaring war. I want to build on the momentum of that message: Love your neighbor, and everyone you meet is your neighbor.

So: Peace, love and understanding. What else?

In a world where a movie called *Godzilla Minus One* can be one of the most beautiful love stories ever committed to film, it's imperative to look for beauty in the most unlikely places. You never know when peace can break out just when you least expect it. Find love —

and if you can't find it anywhere, reach inside and pull it out of your heart.

"What the World Needs Now is Love" is a song written and recorded 60 years ago, and it is still "Now." The world needs love, not just for some but for everyone — again, because everyone is a neighbor.

Let's fill this blank slate with "I love yous."

So: Peace, love and understanding. What else?

"Preface" was the 1,249th consecutive daily post I prepared for this space. The year 2025 begins with the 1,615th. I probably make too big a deal about that streak, and I commit the sin of pride when I think about it. I don't believe I have accomplished anything else for 1,615 consecutive days in a life that has seen more than 26,000 days to date, so I guess it is a pretty big deal.

So: Peace, love, understanding, and try to show up every day. What else?

When you say something to someone, mean it.

Tell the truth, even when it hurts. Your lies will be discovered sooner or later, and you won't like what happens when they are.

Take care of your pets. They are a lifetime commitment. How you treat the animals in your care defines you to others in ways that can't be expressed.

You know that familiar question, "Where do you want to be in five years?" I just looked back at my blog posts to see where I was five years ago.

It turns out I didn't write anything for Jan. 1, 2020. The streak was still eight months in my future. But on Dec. 31, 2019, I wrote about a theme I would later recognize in the DNA of *Godzilla Minus One*: In the face of death, live!

And live like crazy, the way Ray Bradbury wrote about living, as I quoted:

"To live at the top of your lungs, your genetics, the rambling and incoherent half-awake, half-asleep dreams just before dawn, or in the morning shower, or on your pillow during afternoon naps. To

NOT KNOW what you're doing but find out in the doing. To always be surprised and never damn or turn away from surprise. To love life while surrounded by so much that is annihilation. To answer, as I did one night not long ago at a lecture, when asked, 'Why do you write so much about death? To which I said, 'Because I am alive.'"

OK. The slate is no longer blank. The year 2025 is underway for real. Here we go. In some ways it looks just like 2024, but make no mistake, it's becoming its own year second by second, minute by minute.

Isn't this great? And if it isn't, how can we make it so?

Getting better

On New Year's Eve Seth Godin cited an article by a man named Max Rosen that posited, "The world is awful. The world is much better. The world can be much better. All three statements are true at the same time."

It is fairly easy to see on a macro level. Imagine what life was like in 1925, and now 1825, and now 1725, and next 1525, and then 25 A.D. What once was awful is much better 100 years later, over and over, but there was/is always a long way to go.

It's harder to see day by day, but still ... A demented human drives a pickup truck into a crowd on New Year's morning: The world is awful. Billions of people celebrated the new year peacefully and joyfully: The world is better. A handful of people around the world celebrated the disgraceful horror in New Orleans as if it was a victory against the great Satan: The world can be much better.

When I turned the page to what would become my first journal entry of the new year, the Bible verse on the page was a familiar one from Galatians: "But the fruit of the spirit is love, joy, peace, patience, kindness, goodness, faithfulness, gentleness, self-control. Against such things there is no law."

Sometimes when something awful happens, it's easy to believe the fruits of the spirit are nowhere to be seen. But they become easier to spot day by day, and people keep finding and adopting Paul's words as their own — and so the world is much better than it was, even though it can still be much better.

How can we make our worlds better today? It's a constant challenge.

The year the world became better

This was my blog post for Dec. 31, 2022.

New Year's Eve is when the optimists come out to play, with our resolutions and fresh goals and hopes and prayers.

Maybe 1941 will be the year when nations stop rattling swords at each other and sue for peace.

Maybe 1968 will be the year when people stop thinking skin color determines superiority or inferiority.

Maybe 1990 will be the year when we are finally free to beat our swords into plowshares.

Maybe 2020 will be the year when authoritarians grow tired of their games and trust in freedom.

Maybe 2023 will be the year when ... humanity changes its very nature?

The pessimists who call themselves realists are not surprised when humans' basest nature rears its head again and the resolutions and fresh goals and hopes and prayers clatter to the dirt.

We often hang our heads and realize there is no peace on Earth, despite what the bells on Christmas Day say — but there is more peace than there once was. Americans and Japanese and British and

Germans work and play together. People with different skin colors marry, and their families are welcomed with love and acceptance. Around the world, every day, day by day, billions upon trillions of human interactions are performed peacefully, and we are always appalled when violence intervenes. Even the authoritarians are constantly frustrated by the independent thinkers who refuse to kowtow and do things their way.

Maybe last year was not the year when everything changed — but some things changed.

Inch by inch, bird by bird, soul by soul, not all at once but slowly, the world has become a better place than it was one, 10, 50, and 100 years ago.

Maybe this will be the year we finally accept that and are grateful.

Or maybe the calendar doesn't matter, and you and I should simply do what we can to make this day better than yesterday was, day by day.

Happy New Year, friends.

It's all connected – Take 2

A few days before any final revisions were due for this book, a friend helped me with a breakthrough that may have been obvious to everyone except me.

I went on Facebook and posted the shortest chapter, which was called "It's All connected" and read as follows:

It's all connected
I want to write more stories.
I want to learn more stories.
I want to write more songs.
I want to learn more songs.
I want to write more books.
I want to read more books.

My old pal Sam Kujava replied, "I read the word 'want' a lot. As Yoda would reply to Luke, 'There is no want. DO.' But you don't have a Yoda on your back, so you have to motivate yourself. Cheers."

The lightbulb that appeared over my head would have been

blinding if lightbulbs actually appeared over our heads when we get an idea or finally comprehend.

"OMG, all I have to do is eliminate the "I want to" from those six sentences!" I told him.

It's all connected

Learn more stories.
Write more stories.

Learn more songs.
Write more songs.

Read more books.
Write more books.

One leads to the other, you see, and it works in any field. If there's something you want to accomplish, examine how other people have accomplished the same thing and follow their example in your own way.

I feel like Scarecrow and Tin Man — "I should have thought of it for you." "I should have felt it in my heart." Thankfully Sam was there to tell them, "No, he had to find it out for himself. Now those magic slippers will take you home in two seconds!"

Excuse me while I go click my heels together three times.

Snapshot

The 11-year-old dog tries to keep up as the 3-year-old pup growls playfully and romps around the house: "Let's wrestle! Let's run! Let's be pals!"

After a few minutes, the old girl leaps into a chair where the young'un can't reach, then comes over to the love seat for some attention from me.

She pants as I rub her and say, "That's my good girl," and the younger pup sulks across the room, eying the two older beasts with suspicion. Why do the man and her older sister move about so slowly? Don't they know there's a world out there to run around in?

Yes, little one, we know, and nature has slowed us down, but at this more leisurely pace we can see and feel the details of this grand world more easily — the chickadee foraging at the bird feeder, the squirrel dancing from branch to branch, the freshly fallen snow dusting the ground and adding a layer of beauty to the landscape — frosting on a plain cake.

Dejah steps down, and Summer immediately brings over a toy to resume the tug of war. Now it's the old one growling playfully. She is a good sport.

Until you can't

ob Uecker has died. That makes me sad, along with a few
million other folks.

Uecker became the radio voice of the Milwaukee
Brewers in 1971, the same year I landed in Wisconsin, so I've never
known a time when he wasn't there. He became a legendary broad-
caster and so much more.

Just before the new year began, we lost Jimmy Carter, who was a
great man if not a very good president. The first person I recall
using the phrase "born-again Christian" to describe himself, after his
defeat in 1980 he went on to become the best ex-president of my
lifetime.

We revere people who keep doing excellence well into their 80s
and 90s. Not so much politicians who overstay their welcome in the
halls of power, but people like Uecker and Carter, and before them,
Tony Bennett or Betty White. I think of people like Dick Van
Dyke, Willie Nelson, Paul McCartney and Ringo Starr, Mick Jagger
and Keith Richard, Bob Dylan, Neil Young, Joni Mitchell — we
have not lost them yet, but we will someday.

They are my role models. I have set a date to retire from my
longtime day job, but I plan to keep writing and contributing what I
can until I can't.

When colleagues expressed concern about the state of our industry — worried about rumored layoffs and such — I would tell them, "The best we can do is the best we can do until they tell us we can't anymore." I later added, "And even if they tell you that you can't, find a way to keep doing it anyway, because it's not their decision."

My current plan is to keep doing the best I can until I can't anymore, and for now, I still can.

Thanks for the memories, Ueck, and for showing us how it's done.

❦

I'd love to change the world

W hat am I trying to say? What do I hope to accomplish? I am one of 7 (or is it 8) billion humans on this planet — how can little me make any difference at all? I can say or write nothing that someone else hasn't said or written already. Who do I think I am?

But ...

I can make life easier for this dog and that dog. I can spread some seed to feed a few dozen birds this morning. I can give a smile to that man or that woman. I can make a small difference to anyone I encounter today, and try to make it a positive difference.

I can't change the world, but I can make theirs a little better. That's a start.

About this day

Goodness! It's Thursday, January 30, 2025!
What does that mean in the grand scheme of things?
It's only a name we have given this particular day, to differentiate it from any other day in history. Today is not August 15, 1947, nor is it April 17, 1522, but significant things did happen on those days, too. I couldn't tell you what those significant things are, but to the people who were wrapped up in those happenings, it was important.

That's how I know lives will be affected today, because as we pass from here to there, lives change every day. Perhaps it's your turn or my turn — perhaps my writing this passage, or your reading it, will be the catalyst for a slight change in perspective that will lead to a breakthrough. Maybe it will be that intentional, or maybe not intentional at all, but this very day lives will change all over the world.

Couples will conceive babies, babies will be born, loved ones will die, marriages will begin and end, jobs will start, folks will retire — so many ways that January 30, 2025, will be remembered for better or for worse.

Here in the hour before sunrise, the day seems to throb with potential. What will this day bring — something new or same old same old? Nothing special or something unforgettable? As much as you can, try to make it memorable, knowing on the other hand that in a world of billions, it's just as likely that someone else will push this day over into history — personal history or world history.

Just remember to live it like it's once in a lifetime, because we assigned it the name of Thursday, January 30, 2025, because this day is now and will never come again.

February — bah, humbug

F ebruary is the shortest month, thank God. I am not a fan of winter, and February is the depths of winter.

I struggle to say anything nice about February, and my mother always said "If you can't say anything nice ..."

The best thing I can muster to say about February is that by the time it ends, winter is almost over, at least officially. In these parts we see the occasional snowstorm in April or even May, but at least that snow melts rather quickly. Snow is a constant cover in February.

Oh, there's Valentine's Day, a time to celebrate romance, but shouldn't one celebrate one's partner every day year-round? Shouldn't we regularly treat that partner in a way that makes Feb. 14 just another in a long series of days of loving companionship?

Oh, there's the Super Bowl, the grand championship of a sport built for autumn after a series of playoff games, some of them played on frozen fields when most sane human beings are inside warming by the fire. (Don't get me started about winter-sport championships played in June.)

And oh, pitchers and catchers report for spring baseball training in mid- to late February, but at least they have the sense to do so in

Arizona or Florida. Here in the north, that beloved white sphere most likely would just get lost in a snowdrift.

No one writes stories (although maybe someone should, perhaps as a parody) about a cranky codger who thinks February is a humbug but, through a series of supernatural interventions, comes to know the real meaning of February and vows to keep February in his heart all the time for the rest of his life.

In our neck of the woods, the beginning of February means six more weeks of winter, whether or not a rodent sees its shadow, and after that — finally — blessed relief, some years more quickly than others.

And so, here's to February, the shortest month: May it fly by as fast as it can.

What everything means

I sneezed, a most prodigious sneeze that made one dog look up, while the other chased squirrels in her dreams. I looked around the room and dove into thought, wondering if I could find meaning or a turn of a phrase that would shift my musing from the mundane into the eternal. It didn't come just that moment — celestial insights lay somewhere beyond my mind's eye, out of my metaphorical grasp.

I wanted to say once and for all what everything means. In all likelihood, it's not for any of us to know fully. We can find our own purpose, we can decide on a meaning, but I can't say for certain what anyone else's purpose might be, and I can't tell you what any of it means for you.

That's up to you — and isn't that thought powerful? Scary, yes, but think of it: Your fate is in your hands for you to understand and fulfill. And maybe that's the celestial insight I was reaching for.

No one else is in your soul or your body or your mind, so only you can say your purpose with any certainty.

Don't call it scary; call it awesome.

Inside looking out

It was a snow globe day — big white fluffy flakes drifting down from the sky from dawn to dusk. I was able to stay inside most of Saturday, except when I saw that I was out of wild bird seed.

There are two roads to the nearest grocery store — I took the county road there and had to drive patiently at 30 mph, barely noticing how beautiful it all was. The county crews had to focus on keeping the state highway clear, so I took that way home. Even so I needed to go about 55 mph, about 17 mph more cautiously than usual.

I needed to clear the driveway with the snowblower before I went anywhere. I tried going out without snowplowing, but the car slipped and slid and refused to go up the incline to the road, so out came the machine for the first time this winter. That's another reason I am able to wax poetic about this day — we haven't had enough snow this winter for it to be irritating, at least not yet.

As I was slowly negotiating the roads, I found myself wondering if I was crazy for driving 10 miles through a snowstorm for two 20-pound bags of bird seed. But sitting back in my easy chair in 68-degree artificial warmth, I think of the birds and other animals hunkered down out there, for whom my ration of seed will be the only easy thing they receive in the weather, and I decide that it was worth the drive. If I had spun out or had another mishap, I might feel differently about it, but I didn't, and so I will sleep well tonight and feed the birds in the morning.

The best we can do

This is the week I reminded myself that yes, I can fix stuff around the house. With the help of a YouTube video, I was able to replace the broken drain pump in my washing machine, although my natural bent to procrastination kept me from doing the task until almost all of my seasonal clothes had been used up.

The machine successfully ran constantly Wednesday through Friday morning, and now all my clothes are freshly laundered, except for the pajamas I'm wearing and my Thursday ensemble. The vicious circle turns again, but it's back to normal.

It has also been a frustrating week. Summer just isn't eating. An x-ray found stones in her bladder, and the non-surgical solution is a special diet, but remember the part where she just isn't eating? I haven't ruled out a hunger strike, because she's acting normal otherwise. I don't think we're going to have to resort to surgery, Lord willing and the creek don't rise.

All of my life is Lord willing and the creek don't rise, but I don't want the creek rising anytime soon. There is always much worrisome stuff on the horizon, and I've reached that stage in life when mortality looms over everything. I have not fully processed the loss of Red — Mary the Hugger has become a treasured part of my life, but I still miss mon cherie and I guess I always will. Her memory is a constant reminder that endings are inevitable and the creek will someday rise up and overcome us all.

A guy could get bitter — but mostly I see it as a reason to be kind. We are all in the same predicament, so why not Love God and Love Your Neighbor and make it easier on one another while we have the chance?

The best we can do is the best we can do until we can't anymore. That's a brighter and more calming message than it may appear at first glance. It's not a call to mediocrity and not caring how well we live — I did say "the *best* we can do," after all — but knowing all things must pass is a reason to get on with those things and cherish it all while we can, not waste our time on the petty and the mean.

A neighbor might need a hand, so why waste time being angry and outraged over what's out of our control? That serenity prayer is awfully wise advice, and if changing things is going to take courage, then we'd best get on with it — remembering always to do it with a giant dose of love.

Evidence right in front of us

When Summer was a puppy and stairs were a strange and mysterious mystery, I would hook her up to a leash and take her out front to do her doggie business rather than force her to negotiate the 10 steps down from the deck to our fenced-in backyard.

Now closer to her fourth birthday than her third, she has long ago grown accustomed to stairs, but after numerous bouts of hesitation at the patio door, I finally realized that first thing in the morning, she prefers to harken back to her puppyhood and go out front.

Since I am still at least 30 pounds heavier than I would consider my ideal weight, in recent months I have capitulated to my goofy dog's preference and taken her on a 10- to 15-minute walk up and down the road and/or through the big field next to the house. (Summer, Dejah and I live on a little more than three acres of land not far from the beautiful shores of Green Bay — the body of water where the city gets its name.)

One Saturday morning, after my usual morning surf through comic strips, familiar blogs and word games, I dabbled briefly on social media and even stuck my toe into the debate *du jour* involving heads of state. That's a little unusual given that I ultimately view our present crisis as the state versus the individual, rather than any state-versus-state or party-versus-party.

Be that as it may, people took sides and expressed their anger and dismay at whichever head of state they viewed as being mainly at fault. At that point Summer expressed her dismay that we had not gone for our walk yet, so I pocketed the phone and grabbed the leash.

It was a cold but beautiful sunny morning. Sunny days help my depth perception — you may recall the story of when I first got glasses, the doctor added a prism that forced my two eyes to work better together — and so I stopped a time or two just to enjoy the sights of clouds racing across the sky, our three willow trees and the house standing behind them, and the bay peeking through the woods. (For three seasons, you can't see the water from here because of the greenery.)

Summer paused mid-walk and sat down in the field, and I stood next to her and thanked God for a life that has lasted 72 years and brought me to this beautiful corner of the universe. Eventually I coaxed her to continue and we headed back to the house.

I pulled out my phone again and considered leaping back into the fray, but I was pulled up short by a meme a friend had posted. It was a photo of a sunny woods with a river running through it, and these words:

"If you want evidence that the world is a terrible place, watch the news and surf the web. But if you want to remember how incredible this planet is, go out into nature. Unlike social media and the news, nature has no incentive to keep us agitated, angry and anxious."

I reposted the meme and got on with my day, making a point to look out my window and up at the sky as often as possible.

It was a good day.

Marching into a new year

March was the first month I ever saw, although I had no idea what I was looking at.

Of course it's a month of transitions — that's why they put the first day of spring there — but for we who were born in March, the sense of new beginnings is doubled.

It's a schizophrenic month. "March comes in like a lion and goes out like a lamb." Here in these parts the lion came a little early, as we got a five-day streak of heavy snow and high winds that was, frankly, not much fun. The first day of the new month arrives as the calm after the storm.

It's time for the slow crawl out of winter into spring. The crawl can take until May around here — the advice to gardeners is to hold off your planting until Memorial Day. I remember a delightful March with highs in the 60s and 70s that conned me into planting radishes on April 15. The frost on May 3 or 4 took care of those puppies.

We usually have a horrendous snowstorm around mid-March that drops 10 inches of wet snow on us — in 2018 it was 30 inches and mid-April — but then it starts melting almost immediately. I'm hoping this last blast was that storm, a bit early.

Even if it's not, the air is filled with promises of re-emerging life.

The sun has been a more frequent sight, little by little every day. On March 20 the hours of daylight will equal the hours of night, and from that day until September, there'll be more light than dark in the world. Dawn is not as desolate and silent as it was a month or two ago, as the songbirds have started up their music again. And the weather app promises high temperatures above freezing more frequently than not, for the foreseeable future.

When winter strikes in January or February, we turn up our collars and curse the darkness. When winter strikes in March, we smile at the snow and say, "You're not long for this world anyway, nyah nyah nyah."

Daffodils will be warily poking their shoots out of the ground by the end of the month, and we'll soon be checking the dog paws for mud to clean off before they come back into the house. Red has been browsing the seed catalogs and sharing ideas with Wife of Son of Red about their vegetable garden. March 1 brings an air of anticipation that isn't there on February 1.

In many ways this is the "real" new year, the time when nature sheds its blanket and starts to wake again. So, happy new year, and may this March and beyond bring you blessings and love.

A glint of diamond

I believe we can be better than we are, a little bit more every day.

One more second before reacting to that rude person or foolish driver ... one more breath before saying what you feel, just to make sure it really is what you want to say ... one more moment to see every bit of beauty around you, or to see the one glint of diamond in the rough road ahead of you.

We live in a hard world, but it is beautiful; we live in a beautiful world, but it can be hard.

I do not always see the light through the darkness, but when I remember to search for it, I do find it and closer than I realized.

Most of the time, it only takes an extra second.

All we have

Over at a blog I frequent called The Forty-Five one day, quite a conversation broke out after Toirdhealbheach Beucail wrote about how the company that laid him off not long ago has faded into history: When he checked the website, he found a message that said, "Thank you for visiting the website for <Former Employer> ('Company'), a clinical stage biopharmaceutical company formerly based in New Home. The Company is no longer operating."

One of the messages? "... never give the company everything. Because sometimes – it happens to most of us anymore – all of your efforts and emotions and sweat will disappear without a trace," TB said.

Right in the middle of the ensuing discussion, a commentator name Anonymous said:

"All we have in the end are those we love and those who love us."

Yep.

They say no one says on their deathbed that they wish they had spent more time at the office. Nope, when faced with mortality, most of us look around at those we love and those who love us, and gather them close.

Don't wait until mortality calls. Reach out to those you love and those who love you, and hold on with all your might.

And maybe you will fly

Seriously, man, get serious.*

    Don't be frightened. Be excited. Fear and excitement feel like the same sensation anyway, right — a kind of tension and uncertainty? You have no idea if this is going to work, but you may as well try, right?

Would you rather crash and burn or spend the rest of your life wondering, "What if I had jumped off that metaphorical cliff to see if I could fly? Maybe I would have crashed and burned, but what if I had flown?"

Here we are at the precipice, and there is the sky. Yes, there are rocks below, but look at all that sky! What if you tuck the fear and the panic away in a private place and use it as fuel? "I had better get started pursuing my dream, or I might not be able to buy groceries next month," and then work your butt off until you step proudly into the grocery store.

You have an extra booster if you believe in a powerful, loving God. You've heard what He said: With all the beauty in the world, the fields of flowers and the birds in the wild (again, look at all that sky), surely He will take you in the palm of His hand, too, right?

Fear not. Just get down to business. Sure, you're scared, but think of the possibilities if you take flight. Isn't it exciting?

Seriously, man, get serious.*

- - - - -

* "Man" is used in the sense of "Oh, man!" Or "Hey, man ..." If you happen to be a woman, seriously, man, get serious.

Being still

I am almost at the end of my "Be Still" journal. I had three other blank journals waiting, but I picked this one off a store shelf because I felt like I needed the message emblazoned on its cover: "Be still." So, on Page 180 of 192, I ask myself: Have I been still?

"Be still, and know that I am God." Do I sit quietly and wait for that still, small voice enough? Do I dip into The Word enough? Is it "enough" to believe? Is it "enough" to — well, I don't know what "enough" would be.

I do know I often find something delightful when I open the proverbial Good Book. For example — but I can't think of an example just now, which means I have not been in The Word enough lately.

I do know enough to occasionally exclaim, "Thank you, Lord, for this most amazing day!" I do know I might not always hear that still, small voice. As I write this morning, the wind is roaring through the trees and jangling the wind chimes. A thunderstorm is due in a couple of hours, so it will be even harder to hear.

But maybe I do hear something in that wild wind: "I love you so much that I sacrificed my only son so that you can have eternal life, and you know that foul politician who makes you cringe, and that nasty lady in the supermarket, and that murdering terrorist? I love them just as much, and I hope someday you will, too."

Sometimes good news is delivered in a still small voice, and sometimes it roars in the wind. "The heavens declare the glory of God," after all. I guess "Be Still" doesn't have to be literal, and hearing is more about the frame of mind than the volume.

That which governs the dance

My stream of consciousness, as it were, was dammed by the other side of the brain:

"What are you writing?"

"What are you trying to say?"

"What does it mean?"

"What madness will people think overcame you?"

All these questions until the madness was crowded out.

The Self-Editor or the Self-Censor, call it what I may — the governor (I love what that word means, it explains everything), Pressfield's Resistance, Godin's Dip — Every creative seems to have this internal struggle. The poet who flies with inspired not-madness-but-music-that sings-her-soul and is whacked from the sky by those questions even as she soars —

The quotidian — the practical needs of the day — collides with the Transcendence of the Soul in an everyday, ever-spiraling dance.

(I almost wrote "everyday, ever-spiraling fight," but no, the creative soul does not want a fight, seeking not a death struggle, but a dance.)

The words want to dance. The face wants to smile. The chaos wants to sing. Muscles want to relax.

Book shelves are full of dancing souls.

The mind-boggling power
of words and music

And here I go again, looking at the books and records lined up on the shelves and contemplating how many hours or days it would take to read all of the books and listen to all the waiting music.

I think about how long it takes to craft a book and send it to market, and the years spent learning to read and write and play an instrument and combine the playing with other musicians to create a song, and here are hundreds and perhaps thousands of songs and stories surrounding me just in this room.

Many of the souls who created these works have moved on to wherever souls go when their bodies are spent, but their creations remain, and they come alive again when I open the book or play the recording. Our bodies do not live forever, but the words and the music survive and flourish.

What is humanity's greatest invention? I say words, and music close behind. They unite us in ways all other inventions can only approximate. Oh, they can divide us, too, in the wrong hands, but what we have in common is always stronger.

And I mean listen

H ere are three examples of what I mean when I say it's important to take time every day to "listen to music — and I mean *listen*."

• Sometimes the lyrics tell a truth that is so, so real. I never quite grasped the concept of infinity until I heard the line in the great old hymn "Amazing Grace": "When we've been there 10,000 years, bright shining as the sun, we've no less days to sing God's praise than when we'd first begun." Suddenly I realized just how long infinity is.

• Sometimes the words and music combine to describe a feeling perfectly. I love the line in the 1966 song "Cherish" where the guy is trying to find the words to describe how much he cares about the other person.

"Oh, I could say I need you, but then you'd realize that I want you, just like a thousand other guys who'd say they loved you with all the rest of their lies, when all *they* wanted was to touch your face, your hands, and gaze into your eyes." He admits there's a physical attraction, but his feeling is so much deeper than that.

• And sometimes the music doesn't even need words to speak to the heart. I think composer John Williams makes good movies brilliant with his musical scores.

I love listening for the little melodies he attaches to certain characters or objects — there's a moment in *Indiana Jones and the Last Crusade* where he stumbles across a drawing of the Lost Ark of the Covenant, and the score plays just a few notes of the ark's theme from *Raiders of the Lost Ark*.

My favorite John Williams soundtrack is to *E.T. The Extra-Terrestrial*, which is already a sweet story that Williams raises to epic proportions. The movie opens with the title and credits, in purple letters on black over some eerie outer-space-type sounds, but then from the darkness we hear a flute play a six-note theme. On repeat viewings of the movie, after experiencing the places Williams and director Steven Spielberg have taken that theme, just hearing those six notes is all you need to feel the magic all over again.

I like to tell people to watch *E.T.* again and just listen to the music. It's like watching the video of a glorious two-hour symphony.

Just like in the movies, it's easy to let music fade into the background, but music is meant to be heard. That's why I try to find time every day to listen to music — and I mean listen, to hear it.

People say we monkee around

O ne of the mysteries about words and music is that you can listen to a song for 58 years and, one day, hear something you hadn't heard before.

Wandering around the house one morning, I inexplicably began singing "Theme from 'The Monkees'" to myself — you know, "Here we come, walking down the street, we get the funniest looks from everyone we meet ..."

That song has been around since the fall of 1966, but this time a line in the chorus gave me a nudge, sinking in with a smile:

"We're too busy singing to put anybody down."

Isn't that just the way it is with music? You can be mad as hell and ready to blow if you see one more political ad for that crazy person, but put on some music, and you're too busy singing to put anybody down.

Music is a unifying force. Every so often you'll hear an irate musician demand that someone stop playing his or her songs at their political rallies, missing the obvious — that the songs reached across the aisle and made a connection. Instead of cutting that connection, there's an opportunity for understanding — "Tell me what a person like you, who stands for stuff that I can't, heard in that song, and maybe we can find a way to coexist in something more like peace."

It's a cliche to make fun of the cliche of people sitting around the campfire singing "Kumbaya," but it's a basic fact that when you're singing "Kumbaya" or any other song, you're too busy singing to put anybody down.

And hey, hey, that's a good thing.

Morning Song

I need to spend more time with music. Birds sing at dawn; perhaps we should, too. The soft coo of a love song wakes emotions higher than the wail or clamor of an alarm. Who wants to wake from sleep alarmed?

When the heart sings, wounds heal, wrongs are forgotten and forgiven, smiles brighten. When the heart sings, it feels this gift of life in all its wonder and glory. When the heart sings, it draws other hearts to share the music. It's said that misery loves company, but music welcomes company and brings joy to everyone within range of the melody.

Look at me. I have awakened a happier mood in myself simply by writing about music and making an effort to make my words sing. Imagine how I might feel if I actually picked up an instrument or played a recording of music.

The day should start with music. The birds have a better idea.

Words and music

What madness comes over us, after we first learn what letters are, and how they link up to form words, and how the words can connect with each other to express thoughts and tell stories? What is this madness that compels us to commit to this magic process — writing — and say what we need to say and tell what we need to tell over and over?

And what lifts those who read and hear the words to say, "Yes, I feel it, too"? The words connect us in ways only the words can do.

Music takes us one step further, because when we don't speak the same language — and I don't understand your words — we can still share the same lovely tones that soothe our soul or incite us to dance. You may have no idea what neunundneunzig luftballoons are, but we can sing about them together and our spirits are lifted and united.

Words and music — my Lord! Words and music will convey the love and the kindness and the mercy. Oh, yes, sour men and women will counter with words and music of discord — unlike words, though, discordant music can be fun, especially if you can dance to it. Pity the sour men and women who cannot hear the heartbeat of life flowing in every one of us.

I pray for the words and music that will soften the hearts of even the sourpusses, because I love my neighbors, and everyone I meet is my neighbor.

April fools us all

J ust when the showers convince us
          winter is finally over,
          the rain turns to snow.

Just when the snow discourages us,
     the sun comes out
     and melts it all away.

Just when we're ready for laughs and pranks,
     Something serious happens —
     a Titanic sinking,
     a Hitler born,
     a Waco massacre.

April fools us all.

Daffodil shoots lift toward the sky

but must endure a late freeze.

Once April 30 comes along,
    it's all getting greener,
    the lakes and streams resume their flowing,
    and the sky even seems bluer.

In the end, April balances in the positive,
    and it's fun to be outdoors again.
    But meanwhile,

April fools us all.

What April snow showers bring

A nd here came another little round of snow — the talking heads called it snow "showers" and it didn't last long. Snow in April can be unpleasant, but more than in any other month (except perhaps May) it does not feel like a threat — even when the power goes out — because we can be assured it is an anomaly. When it snows in January there's an implied threat of cold and inconvenience for months to come, but the first week in April? This will be melted in a few days and the daffodils and robins can go back to declaring spring.

I plan to plant wildflowers this spring, and zinnias, and oh, some onions and tomatoes. After a year of mourning, I want Three Willows to come alive again in honor and memory of the mistress of this land.

For today, though, we sit in the house and watch the snow make hollow and empty promises, winter's last gasp. When it felt like early spring in early March, some of us were hopeful but not fooled, and this latest storm did not surprise us.

Confusing the old adage, April has come in like a lion. I will be surprised if April does not end with weather fit for a lamb.

It's beginning to look a lot
more like spring

We found the old tricycle at the bottom of our hill that leads to the bay of Green Bay. Like many bits of yard debris, it has rusted away to uselessness but retains an odd charm. We've given it a special place in the garden in front of the house. We were able to measure winter's last gasp last week by the way the snow covered it nearly completely, but as springlike temperatures and rain erased the white stuff, we watched the tricycle re-emerge over the past few days.

And now we can watch the land coming back to life. I noticed a few green sprigs among the grey and brown as Summer and I took a morning walk. It won't be long before the green overwhelms the decay — I didn't specifically look for daffodil shoots, but they must be there. It's their time.

There's no sign yet of the Mayflowers that always erupt next to our garden shed, but hey, it's only April 5.

And that expanse of brown that the tricycle melts into? Believe me, the reason Red placed that charming relic there is because the rust offers a contrast to the explosion of color in that garden every summer. Hold that thought, and I'll post an appropriate example in a few weeks.

As I write this, thunder is rumbling away and rain is blasting down — rain, from the same sky that was dumping snow less than a week ago. It's the season of change, and if you believe in life and growth, it's a good change.

I'm not saying we're free of winter — I'll always remember the 30-inch snowfall of mid-April 2018 — but things are looking up.

Green is my favorite color

I was born on the third day of spring 1953, 50 hours after the vernal equinox, and so the world was green when I first interacted with it. I wonder if that's why green is my favorite color. "What's your favorite color, little boy?" grownups would ask as if they just had to know. "Green!" I would shriek and grab the Crayola crayon. (I probably didn't actually shriek, but) I do remember having an enthusiasm for green.

("Except I remember you pronouncing it *gleen*!" adds my favorite cousin. "Yeah, I knew you then.")

As rain and sun draw the green out of the soil and push the brown and gray away for another season or two, I can feel that enthusiasm come back. It's as though green makes the world right again, renews its energy and restores my soul.

Everyday Blessings

T he pastor said a prayer about remembering our everyday blessings Sunday morning, and I flashed back to the first hour I spent in Wisconsin 53 years ago.

I lived in New Jersey for the first 18 years of my life, and I wanted to go to college somewhere far away, but not as far as my older brother, who went to the University of North Dakota and sometimes sounded lonely out there.

It was for the adventure of it, by the way. New Jersey gets the proverbial bum rap. It was a fun place to grow up, even if it has twice the population of Wisconsin crammed into a fraction of the the land area. I enrolled in Ripon College sight unseen so that I could take a long journey, not to get away from my starting point.

Still, Newark International Airport probably does play a role in this story. It was a dreary August day in Newark — in my memory it was overcast but I can't remember if it was actually raining — and my last breaths before boarding the plane were tainted with jet fuel and smog.

The flight to Milwaukee was above the clouds, of course, and the next leg of the trip was on a wonderful old North Central Airlines prop jet from Milwaukee to Wittman Field in Oshkosh. There, two intensely cheerful Ripon upperclassmen met several of us new freshmen to shuttle us the last 20 miles to the campus in a charming little town.

It was on that last stretch of state Highway 44 that I fell in love with Wisconsin. In contrast to where my travels had started, the air was clear as we drove through a bright sunny day under a huge impossibly blue sky, and everything was green. In my mind's eye all I see are green cornstalks as high as an elephant's, and a pretty big elephant at that.

I like to tell people I decided during that 20-mile drive that I would spend the rest of my days in Wisconsin. I'm sure it wasn't quite that immediate, but I can say it's still my favorite first impression of all the places I've seen. And certainly four years later, when I didn't have a job a week before graduation and faced moving home to New Jersey, I was panicked because the words "home" and "New Jersey" didn't seem to fit in one sentence anymore.

My mind went back to that first day when the pastor prayed that we be grateful for everyday blessings, because after living under that huge impossibly blue sky for 53 years, even that sort of beauty fades into the background. The prayer pulled it back into the foreground, and I spent the rest of the day paying attention.

In fact, I stopped by my car and looked up in the church parking lot, because Sunday was a bright sunny day just like that first one, and the sky was just as big and just as impossibly blue. "Everyday blessings," I said out loud. "Thanks, Lord."

The sweetest communion

I think a real man approaches lovemaking with the sole intention of making the person he loves feel loved. It's not about "having" or possessing someone; it's all about sharing. The times I felt my partner was not wholly satisfied, I was disappointed in myself.

Over time I realized that true intimacy is in that sharing, not in the act that we usually mean when we use the word *intimacy*.

Two songs come to mind — Silly, perhaps, but the first is "I Want to Hold Your Hand." I remember the first time I held a girl's hand — it was electric, even spiritual. When I sing the song, I slow it way down to emphasize the words and that feeling: "When I touch you, I feel happy inside."

The other is Judee Sill's "The Kiss," which captures the yearning and the "sweet communion" of touching lips together. "Love, rising from the mists/Promise me this and only this/Holy breath touching me like a wind song/Sweet communion of a kiss."

As we grow older, it's easy sometimes to overlook the magic of these simplest acts of physical love.

The last advice I ever asked of Red — though I didn't know in the moment that it was the last — was whether I should post the following description of what became the most intimate moments we shared. "Tell me if this is too personal," I asked her, 36 hours before she left us, and read the blog post out loud.

With more energy than I thought she had left, she said simply, "Warren, You have to post that." And so I did, and it bears repeating.

The gentle power of the ponytail

When I visit Red at the hospice, I usually get behind her and pull on her hair, running my fingers through it over and over and massaging her head and shoulders. It's a little ritual she calls "giving her a ponytail," and we have been performing this calming, intimate act together for many years.

Three times during her first few weeks here, three different women came up and told us how beautiful it was to see me stroking her hair like that. I wasn't sure what to say except, "Thank you," but it got me thinking about this relationship between men and women.

My first thought was to let my fellow males know that passionate kisses and wild love-making may reach their woman's heart, but she's more likely to melt in your arms if you brush her hair for awhile. I know she inspires you to urgent passions, but you may get a deeper response with a gentler intimacy.

Red's response to the women's compliments has been a warm acknowledgement and kind of a pride in the fact that this guy belongs to her, and it warms my own soul to hear that pride in her voice. When all is said and done, all a man really wants is to make his lady happy, and so, it appears, mission accomplished.

Let that be a lesson to you, young man.

One day to live

I wonder how our lives might change if we took the perspective that we only have this one day to live.

It a very real sense, today is in fact all we have. That's why it's called reality — only this moment is real. We can't touch the past, though we remember it, and we don't know the future, no matter how much we plan.

All we have is this moment — the birdsong outside the window, the drone of machines coursing up and down the hill or flying overhead, the breathing of the other occupants in the home, the dust and dirt to remove.

All of it, right here in this moment. What shall you do with this moment that is here and now and all around you?

As for me, I will pause and look about and listen and breath, to get my bearings, and soon I will get up from the chair and see what I can do.

I almost wrote, "I will get up from the chair and see what happens," but that implies that I'm just a spectator. If this moment is all I have, I think I would rather be doing.

Cycle

Every morning we are resurrected from the small death, emerge from the cocoon our dying self made the night before, and crawl about gaining our senses.

We wander about performing tasks, learning what we can about this crazy world, and finding ways to entertain ourselves and perhaps others.

All too soon darkness falls. If we are wise, we take some time at the end to reflect on this 15- to 18-hour life and perhaps we leave notes for our next self to find.

Then we make a cocoon, wrap ourselves in it, and yield to the small death, thankful for a day survived and a new life awaiting in the morning.

Trust Monday

Not long after my beloved Red died, I was in Hobby Lobby because — actually, I have no idea why I was in Hobby Lobby. I can't always say I knew what I was doing in those days.

In any case, my brain was in a bit of a whirl until I spotted a wall plaque that said, "I trust the next chapter because I know the author." Those words spoke to me, so I pulled out my wallet and took it home.

You have heard it said, "Monday Monday, can't trust that day." I am here to tell you, yes you can.

I trust Monday because I know the author of days, and He once said, "I know the plans I have for you, plans to prosper you and not to harm you, plans to give you hope and a future."

And so I'm here to tell you, who might be weary or afraid or otherwise just not looking forward to Monday — The Creator of Days has you in His hands. You have reason to hope and a future, and who knows? This Monday could be all you hoped it would be.

Ripples in the wine

Some time ago, I leaned over the plastic communion cup to contemplate the "blood of Christ" thing, holding the cup between the thumb and forefinger of my hand.

As I stared at the grape juice, stock still, I noticed little ripples in the liquid. Even though I wasn't moving, and my hands weren't shaking, the juice was. I realized my beating heart was rushing my own blood through my fingers, and the grape juice was pulsing along with it.

I stared even harder at the cup in awe, with a new understanding beyond my ability to put into words.

Since then, whenever I take communion at church, I pay attention to the ripples in the juice and pray my heartbeat is in sync with the Christ's.

Welcome to Three Willows

Before we even built the house, we stuck three sticks in the ground. The other day, I took a photo from atop our septic mound, and I saw the magnificent trees that our sticks have become, I thought of the name for our 3.33 little acres of paradise: Three Willows.

They say you shouldn't name a stray puppy unless you want to keep it. Does that apply to 3.33 acres of paradise, too? If so, I guess I plan to stay here forever.

There are plenty of worse alternatives. Three Willows sits along the frontage road that used to be what is now the four-lane highway uphill from us. But downhill! There is the approximately one-acre field that I named Willow's Field long ago because of the way our beloved golden retriever loved to run and retrieve her orange disc — I called it The Ting as in, "Get The Ting!" and she would do it over and over tirelessly.

About another acre, sloping downward, is a lovely little woods of about an acre, and down below is a wetland. The land is pie-shaped, and the point of the pie is 150 feet, more or less, from the waters of Green Bay. Because of the woods you can only see the bay in the winter, but you can certainly hear it on a windy night!

It took 11 years of living memories to come up with the name, but it feels like it fits. And so, welcome to Three Willows.

Compass plants reach for the sky

Probably my favorite wildflowers here at Three Willows are the compass plants, so named because supposedly their leaves always point north.

For two years I thought the compass plant was a bit of a bust. It had big interesting leaves, but that just made it kind of a fun little bush. I guess it takes some time for compass plants to mature to the point where they flower, and that third year made up for the boring beginning.

For the first few weeks, the then-lone compass plant showed its floppy leaves, same as always, but then one day a stem shot up about eight feet in the air, and a few days after that a half-dozen blossoms burst out. Talk about your ugly duckling transforming into a swan!

The flowers drop seeds as those long stems droop at the end of the summer, and after a few years we have compass plants all over the wildflower gardens. Between the compass plants and the cup plants — who deserve their own story one of these days — the field is a glorious display of green and gold, which is a lovely and appropriate sight not far from the shore of the bay of Green Bay.

Pelican beauty

My day job took me one Sunday to three communities where thousands of people gathered for fun, and according to my smart phone I took more than 10,000 steps in a day for the first time in memory.

As I pulled into the driveway I thought to myself, "I'm so tired, I just want to go to bed early tonight, but I still need to write a blog entry."

I stepped out of the car and looked up. More than 50 pelicans were flying overhead in a V formation.

I love watching pelicans fly in groups. They are so elegant and graceful and seemingly relaxed as they drift on the air.

It's always worthwhile to stop and smell the roses, or even better to look up and see the pelicans.

Eagles fly like, well, eagles

I remember the first time I saw an eagle flying overhead at our retreat not far from the shores of Green Bay, a few years ago now. It was heart-stoppingly beautiful, that majestic bird fighting back against extinction and soaring along.

Friday afternoon I sat down on the bench in Willow's Field and looked up to see nine of them. I think they were all eagles; I only spotted one white head among them, but it takes quite a bit of time for a young bald eagle to attain that distinctive look.

They were dancing in the wind, sometimes flying near each other, sometimes spreading out, always following the breeze or using it to soar higher or slide lower.

"Huh," I said, "that's a lot of eagles."

I realized then that they have become commonplace in our neck of the woods, so commonplace that I don't stop to watch unless there are a whole bunch of them playing together in the sky.

How wonderful it is that I have misplaced my sense of wonder over the miracle of these majestic beasts.

The pelicans have not returned yet from wherever they go during the very cold weather. I look forward to seeing them again. It wasn't so very long ago that you didn't see pelicans around here at all.

No doubt some political-minded someone will claim credit for bringing eagles and pelicans to the Green Bay area with some rule or another. I'm just glad to see eagles and pelicans cavorting overhead.

I knew that smile

The girl was new at this. She rolled down the slight incline of her driveway, suddenly perhaps realizing that she could possibly roll into the path of my oncoming car. Then she rotated her arms wildly in the way people do when desperately trying to maintain their balance, and finally she stepped off the skateboard.

She smiled sheepishly at me as I drove past, and, in the instant before my glimpse of her ended, I saw her smile inwardly at herself.

She's going to be all right.

The smile said, "I don't have this yet, but I will have this. It's funny that that guy saw me fall short, but we both know I will get this."

No doubt, after I was out of sight, she stepped back on the skateboard and said to herself, "You got this."

We see the Olympic snowboarder or skateboarder defy gravity. We never see the thousands of times she fell or the hundreds of smiles she smiled at herself after she had to flail her arms to keep her balance.

We see the all-star quarterback throw the tight spiral into the arms of his sprinting receiver 25 yards downfield. We never see the thousands of times he didn't.

"You got this," they say to themselves after they fall short. And eventually, if they keep trying, they do.

Writing and the joy of running off-leash

Summer and I have begun taking walks through our land of late. For now I have to keep her leashed, but I try to let her lead the way for the most part.

We may wander near our wildflowers, up and down the septic mound, or as we did Wednesday morning, through the woods. Summer was most intrigued by an old plastic Adirondack-style chair, which we used to sit in, but is now well on its way to being more or less reclaimed by Ma Nature.

Dean Wesley Smith wrote the other day about walking through a mall and seeing a couple of toddlers delighting in the exploration of it all, with their mothers watching carefully but smiling at their kids' fun. One ran over and lovingly petted a stone elephant. Smith used it as a metaphor for the creative process.

The kids are the creative voice, having fun running this way and that and finding new ways to love life in every corner, and the moms are the critical voice, keeping a watchful eye out that the kids don't get in trouble but, for today, letting them run and play.

"So next time you sit down at your writing computer, just let the creative voice run and play and pet the stone elephants. You might be surprised at how much fun you have writing and how good what you write turns out to be (if you leave it alone.)"

Perhaps Summer is her own metaphor for the creative process.

As she and I amble through the woods, Summer sometimes wants to run like the wind and I have to hold the leash with both hands. Sometimes she stops to sniff an old tree or nibble on some grass a little too long, and I give her a little tug. She may willingly yield and come along with me, or she may stand her ground and keep sniffling.

I look forward to the day when, like her beloved predecessor, I can just step outside with Summer and she will run and play and sniff and chase off-leash, because I can trust her to come back to me when I call her.

There is a feeling here that the day I let my creative juices off the leash is when the real magic will start happening. But, to extend the metaphor, before you can fly and be free you must first learn how to fly. Summer must learn how to stay in the yard before she can be free to run around the yard.

They say the great improvisational musicians know their instruments and the music so well that they can soar off the written page and create something new and inventive on the spur of a moment. If I want to write something that perhaps breaks the rules and takes the reader to a whole new place, I first need to know what the rules are and master working within those rules.

Those kids and Summer (the creative voice) will someday run and play without Mom or the leash (the critical voice) needing to hold them back. And what a day that will be.

And the music is still everywhere

"I want to live," the soul says with every fiber of its being. "I want to soar. I want to fly. I want to dance. I want to feel. I want to run, I want to sit still and drink all this in, I want to swim, I want to float quietly in the sunlight."

When the soul says, "I want to die," it doesn't really. It's folded into despair so deep until it believes peace can't be found in this life. It knows there is soaring to be done somewhere, and maybe in the next plane of existence, the soul can dance.

But the music is here, and the dance is at hand. Listen. Move your feet. Breathe. See that? You're dancing.

The song is everywhere if you just listen. All around you are wind and melody and rhythm, everywhere.

And the words to every song are, "I want to live."

So what's stopping you? Live!

Oh! August

August has no holidays because August is a holiday all its own.

The summer flowers are ablaze, and the summer warmth borders on heat, and the birds cross the sky, and who needs a holiday to love all of this?

Yes, I know on the other side of the world it's darkest winter — or at least so I've heard, I've never been on the other side of the world, but I've been in darkest winter, and I can imagine there is an opposite place somewhere, where a place much like ours is covered in fallen snow and the mild temperatures of now are bitter and chilling. And no doubt the people there think of August the way we think of February.

But oh! August! Sweet warm August! With your dash of cold morning dew reminding us you are not here to stay — but nothing stays in this world, does it? So we love and rejoice in the moment, thankful that such moments drift by a respite from all the chaos, a clarity in the midst of the mist, a promise that peace is possible — a possibility of possibilities.

Interplanetary travel from the back deck

I let the dogs out for one last constitutional before bed and stood on the deck overlooking our back yard. The air was room temperature — 68 degrees according to the weather app — and filled with the sound of crickets and other nighttime singing creatures. Everything was green and summer-lush.

I tried to imagine the same scene absolutely quiet, the air so cold I need to wear a coat even for just a few minutes, and the ground covered with a deep layer of snow, everything white and gray.

In my head I know it's possible — not only possible but completely likely, because I have been here and under those conditions time and time again. In the middle of summer my heart screams no, it can never be — just as it does when I stand in the cold and try to imagine a lush, green night full of life sounds.

The cycle of the four seasons is a fascinating phenomenon. Just as we live different lives within the span of "one" lifetime, we live in four different worlds by staying in the same place, year after year.

And on the first day

One dog licked her back paw, the other chewed a bone. The washing machine whirred from the next room. It was the first day of the rest of his life.

He scoffed under his breath. "Cliche much?" he muttered. But it was true. He had awakened very much aware of his mortality. His neck ached. He walked slowly and gingerly through the house. His body, never particularly athletic or toned, felt worn.

He had listened while Bob Goff read his book *Everybody, Always* over the last couple of days. It was a book about love and forgiveness and the supernatural power of Christ, and overcoming through persistence and that forgiveness and love.

"Persistence," he scoffed, thinking of his lack there. Still, today was the first day of the rest of his life.

He remembered writing about the second day, a long time ago — how if you stumble on the first day, then you can start on the second day of the rest of your life, or on the third day, and all you've lost are a couple of days.

Or — and the insight crashed against him like an ocean wave on a windy day — was the idea all along to treat every day like the first day? The first day of any new venture is full of promise and hope and energy and "You can do this" because nothing has gone wrong

— perhaps a little bit of anxiety because it's new and unknown, but there's all the excitement of a new beginning, a new hope, a new direction.

"Today is the first day ..." and it's always today. Every day is a new first day, a new promise, and a new hope.

Every day is the first day of the rest of your life — and suddenly he was excited, and he knew how to live, and to love. He wasn't sure he could be that refreshed and ready every day, but it was the anxious optimism of the first day on the job, the eagerness of the first day of vacation, and the joyousness of a wedding day. It was the discovery of a cliche turned over and examined to find a new meaning, perhaps its intended-all-along meaning.

He saw at last, and every day became the first day from then on.

what comes to you in the silence

Some of the work I'm proudest of didn't get a single "Like" on my blog or on Facebook.

Austin Kleon shared Michaela Coel's Emmy acceptance speech where she spoke of how "visibility these days seems to somehow equate to success" and added, "don't be afraid to disappear from it, from us, for a while and see what comes to you in the silence."

Kleon then added, "Silence is a space for something to happen." It often is enlightening to step away from the electronics and all the stimulation and turn off the brain or present myself with a blank page and see what fills that space.

I just stopped and looked through the window of my room here, not far from the shores of Green Bay, and a lone bird flew across the little bit of sky I can see above the trees, probably a gull, maybe a pelican, but high enough that I couldn't be sure, and alone enough that I wondered if it was lost and seeking its friends — Do birds have friends? colleagues? fellow travelers? They have mates, of course, but what else do we really know?

Where I was going before the bird flew across my consciousness is how right Coel's comment felt. Something special might be waiting in the silence when you disconnect, when you dare something that might not immediately gather those precious Likes. A swarm of clicks can be satisfying, but so can that connection that, for now at least, is only within.

Why does it have to be September?

The days run by, and suddenly it's a month with withering flowers and changing-color leaves in it. September is still summer, as schoolchildren are forced to forget, and the days promise warmth and sunshine and a bit of sass, same as July, but night and the edge of consciousness bring a creeping coolness and an early sunset.

God says, "Don't be afraid, I'll paint the world with vivid colors as my promise that the sun and warmth will be returning, and in the coldest months the days will grow longer again and it will be spring and summer again before you can say 'Bob's your uncle' or wonder what that means."

All of that flashes through the mind when "September" appears on the calendar. It's a bittersweet feeling, bitter because you remember how the hint of coolness turns into struggling against the snow and the sharp edges of the cold, sweet because there's so much summer left, and after that the comforting embrace of falling leaves and matching sunsets and hordes of geese honking through the air as if to say, "See you in the springtime, friends, and thanks for watching out for our kids as they fluffed out and grew."

Why does it have to be September? You might as well wonder

why you have to live and breathe. There are cycles of warm and cold, bitter and sweet, because it's all a cycle, all of it. Embrace the cycle and work with it and play with it; that's the sanest way to live. Accept what you can't change, and fight for what you can.

The Fable of Any Road

I t's a wind chime day, and it rained last night and looks to rain some more. The leaves are still green, mostly, and the Black-eyed Susans are still gathered, perhaps fading at the edges. Barely one week left in summer, or so says the calendar, but in this part of the world, summer can be fleeting and the darker months linger past their welcome.

I don't mind a dreary day. It makes the warm coffee more special, and comfort food has a chance to fulfill its purpose. My mind wants to fill my conscience with a list of things I could have done all summer, but there's still a scoonch of summer left to do some of it, and the rest can wait. I see the list of all I did do, and that will have to be enough. I can't call back the summer anyway and, Lord willing, I'll have another season for those tasks left undone.

I must remember to be more intentional, to set an agenda for the new day's action, and follow it as best I can. Too many days I fritter away aimlessly, thinking, "I wonder what I can do today, only to reach sunset and think, "Oh yeah, oh no, I know what I could have done."

There's always tomorrow, I think at that point, but then another aimless day comes and goes. I find that if I set a plan in stone, I resist its merciless face, but a plan too flexible is a wet noodle with no power or fire at all.

"Where are you going, young man?" the old man asked along the way.

"I don't really know," said the young man.

"You're in luck, or maybe not," replied the old man. "Any road will take you there."

"I've heard that one before," the young man scoffed. "It sounds so wise, but a long and winding road gives me time to enjoy the scenery along the way."

"Absolutely," the old man agreed. "You can even double back if you decide you passed your real destination. Just try not to regret the days you could have been spending settled there. The journey is as rewarding – more so, really – than the final stop."

"That's what I'm saying."

"Still, a bit of finding where you want to go beats meandering, and that's all I'm saying."

And what do you know, the young man set his sails that day and discovered it was so.

Stand still, look around and pay attention

L ate summer nighttimes, here near the shores of Green Bay, are noisier than late winter nighttimes, if only for the crickets. Their ancient song is comforting, an echo of late summer nighttimes I've heard for all my life. Poets who died before I was born wrote about the lovely sound of crickets singing in the night, as no doubt poets will write who are born after I die.

A gentle breeze nudges the wind chimes under my window, a melody I've written about before but have not listened to in a few weeks. Why, I wonder, do we sometimes ignore the beauty that we see and hear every day. As Dorothy said when she returned to Kansas (I paraphrase), we can find what we're looking for just by standing still, looking around and paying attention.

My beloved cup plants and compass plants are fading, their yellow blossoms shriveling and drooping, as bittersweet a sight as their arrival in early August was sweet. Fifteen-ish years ago we planted a half-dozen cup plants and three compass plants among the native plants we purchased in hopes of creating a field of wildflowers, and the cup plants number in the hundreds these days.

The compass plants have been slower to spread. For the first two years they didn't bloom at all, but then that third year, one or two shot stems taller than I am (73.25 inches) with starburst yellow flowers. There were at least two dozen of those flowery stalks, probably more, this summer.

I used to be more interested in growing vegetables than in flowers, although I admired the blooms my partner coaxed out of the ground all over our land. Lately I've begun to appreciate the spontaneous beauty of a flower in the wild.

"Beauty is truth, truth beauty,—that is all Ye know on earth, and all ye need to know," John Keats wrote in his "Ode On A Grecian Urn." The same could be said of the flowers. A botanist could tell us how they fit into the biosphere, but as far as their utility for us humans is concerned, it seems they exist mainly to be beautiful. That, my friend, is a fine purpose indeed.

The beauty of the
southern Door peninsula

R
ed and I watched two dozen pelicans testing the wind currents. As we watched from our lawn chairs in front of the garage, they rose higher and higher and farther and farther away, until they were white glints of sunlight that blinked as they flew in and out of our field of vision.

On a windy day like today, the crashing waves of Green Bay can be heard just beyond the trees. Of course, this is autumn, and so it won't be very long until our water view returns. We can't see the bay through the leaves from April to October.

Most people think of Green Bay as the smallest city in the National Football League and have no clue about the grand body of water that gives the community its name. In the 1991 movie Bingo, the story of a dog and a Green Bay Packers football player, the film-makers used the massive metropolis of Pittsburgh with its mighty Pennsylvania mountains to stand in for Green Bay, the city. Not. Even. Close.

Green Bay, the city, grew at its southern shores. The bay extends 120 miles north, bounded on the west by Northeast Wisconsin and Upper Michigan and on the east by the Door Peninsula, a string of small islands known collectively as the Grand Traverse, and Michigan's Garden Peninsula. Lake Michigan lies beyond.

So the land where we chose to settle is a narrow peninsula with Green Bay on the west and Lake Michigan on the east, and people come by the hundreds of thousands to see its remarkable vistas – especially from April to October. The quiet time approaches.

Most of those visitors rush past the "Welcome to Door County" sign and don't believe they are really in Door County until they cross the Sturgeon Bay bridges into Northern Door. They don't know what they are missing.

The wide open farm country and big skies of Southern Door and northern Kewaunee County are not unique to Wisconsin except in their context. Most of the big spaces in Wisconsin are not that close to big waters. The majesty of Lake Michigan and Green Bay makes the Door Peninsula a travel destination but also a magnificent place to live.

When I first started working here, I told people it never felt like I was commuting to work as much as going on vacation like so many other drivers around me. When we built our house here four years ago, moving in was moving home. The entire peninsula is a place to rest, recreate and recharge, and a home here is a personal rest station inside a comfort zone.

People come here to fly and test the wind currents, filling their souls with light so they can face what waits for them back in the real world. I haven't seen most of this planet so I can't personally vouch that it's the most magical place on the planet, but it sure has enough magic to share.

And now, October

If you wait until Oct. 1 to turn on the furnace in these parts, you may be chilly for a few days. We held out until Sept. 28 this year — close enough.

October is the month of brilliant colors, nature's final fireworks display until the drab of bare trees and white and cold, which brings a different kind of beauty, stark and silent.

This is the month of crunchy leaves underfoot, and kids and dogs romping through carefully raked piles, scattering it all over again; the smell of burning leaves (unless banned by people who forget their childhood); the aroma of mulled cider; and the displays of scary and jolly pumpkin faces and skeletons and funny monsters and not-so-funny monsters, topped off by an eerie parade of costumed children in an everlasting quest for bags and bags of chocolate (a quest that never quite ends, as older folks may attest).

October is a month of endings, and growing cold, and creeping darkness in the morning and late afternoon. When dawn begins at 5 a.m. and sunset comes around 9 p.m. and light rules the sky, October is a distant memory — but when it comes around again, it's not as bad as it seemed from that distance. There is a cozy feel to snuggling against the coolness, slippers and sweaters and sweatshirts coming out of storage as old friends. Without October we have no buffer between summer and the winter to come; without the winter to come, we would not appreciate the warmth of the summer sun and we might even curse the heat.

October is our time of battening down the hatches and making sure our defenses against cruel Mother Nature are all in place.

And how could I forget that October is the month when hot chocolate becomes appropriate again? The everlasting quest is fulfilled.

Cacophony pre-dawn

I am sitting on the love seat with my laptop, doomscrolling, when the background sound encroaches on my consciousness: Mixed in with the woosh of tires rolling along the Highway to Paradise up the hill, the cries of hundreds of Canada geese launching into the sky for their journey to wherever it is they go when they're not nesting near the waters of Green Bay.

It's a forlorn, wistful sound — "Goodbye! Goodbye! Take care! Goodbye!" over and over as bird after bird takes to the sky and they take their positions in V after V after V. Of course, sunrise is still nearly an hour away, so the sound is all that carries through the air, and we can only imagine the bustling Grand Central Station of it all.

It's part of the fall, this great migration, this cacophony of leaving, and the sky will become as quiet as it is cold for the next few months. I already know the sound that will break the silence and declare, "We made it! And now spring." It will be the trill of a red-winged blackbird, back from wherever the blackbirds go. Sure as daffodils poking up to defy the frozen soil, the blackbirds' return will signal the end of winter.

I'm getting ahead of myself. First the leaves must finish falling, then the snow must fall and cover the earth for many weeks, and we must endure the silence.

I ache, listening to the geese's cries fading in the sky, but I know, Lord willing, I will hear those cries again, this time a cacophony of "Here we are! Here we are!" as the green creeps back and life starts over again, sometime around my birthday in March, six (!) months on from here.

For now, though, it's "Here we go! Here we go! Goodbye!" and I'm grateful I took the time to stand on the deck and listen and to see them on their way, at least in my mind's eye.

For moments like this, the word *cacophony* was coined.

Gales

November is a stark month. October comes in all green and glorious with a tinge around the edges. Then it flares into reds and yellows and golds, then browns, and then the leaves fall in a heap to reveal stark November.

It's cold and gray, and when the clouds clear away and the sun shines for a day or two, blue is the only color Mother Nature is willing to share — the brown leaves and gray clouds and black nights seem feeble after the wondrous colors of spring and summer and early autumn. Now it's mostly stark and dreary, except perhaps at sunrise or sunset.

We live in the country, so November brings the pop-pop-pop of hunters seeking meat during this time of year when wild animals are fair game. The chill in the air sends us indoors to cozy shelters and warm cider and hot chocolate and bundling blankets, and the sun becomes an occasional visitor instead of a constant companion.

But it's also a time of thanksgiving as we gather around the table and share fellowship and gratitude for the people and the comfort in our lives, and we think of those less fortunate and share of the bounty as we can.

After months of emerging and basking in the great outdoors, November is a time of coming inside. I can appreciate folks who love the cold and enjoy the frigid outdoors — the skiers and the ice fishing enthusiasts and such – but I am content to shrink from the cold and enjoy the warmth of a cozy shelter.

November is the beginning of the cold season, with its gales and its starkness, a time to appreciate the harvest, settle in for a long time of mostly indoors, and be grateful for all that we have.

Wait, warm cider? hot chocolate?

I love November.

Footsteps

Nov. 15, 2020

I was listening to the soundtrack of "Springsteen on Broadway" on Saturday when the rock star/singer-songwriter got to talking about his dad.

"When I was a young man and looking for a voice to meld with mine, to sing my songs and to tell my stories, well, I chose my father's voice, because there was something sacred in it to me," Springsteen said. "When I went looking for something to wear, I put on a factory worker's clothes, because they were my dad's clothes, and all we know about manhood is what we have seen and what we have learned from our fathers, and my father was my hero and my greatest foe."

I wonder if all boys want to follow in their father's footsteps, to live up to the man they believe he is, and I think probably so. I know I've always tried to treat women the way my father treated my mother, because he set such a good example. My father was an electrical engineer and a ham radio operator, and watching him throw his voice hundreds of miles with that mysterious array of humming machines probably had something to do with my choosing radio as my medium during the first half of my career.

My father was not an overly demonstrative man, but we never felt unloved, not by our parents at least. I remember one angst-filled night when, certain to the depths of my teenage soul that I would always be alone and misunderstood, I fled from the dinner table to my room and threw myself sobbing onto the bed, dimly aware that I was being ridiculously melodramatic but unable to withdraw from the youthful crazy. My dad came in and sat on the bed beside me, no doubt feeling at a loss himself, and he rested a hand on my shoulder and sat there as long as I needed. He didn't say a word, and he didn't have to. He was just there, and that was all it took.

I wrote about that moment in a newspaper column to thank him on his 80th birthday. The only conversation we ever had about that column was on the phone a few days later when I paused for an awkward moment and asked him if he saw it. "Yes," he said, "It was nice," and then there was another awkward pause, and that was how we knew how meaningful it was for both of us.

My father was born on this date 97 years ago, and for the first time since 1923 he's not around to be celebrated. His father lived to be 85, and none of his four siblings made it to 90, so it was a pleasant surprise when he completed his ninth decade. "You may as well hang around to make it to 100," I said, and he laughed and said something like, "We'll see." Mom died when they were both 82, and the last time I talked with him about her, he looked me in the eye and said, "I miss her," with as much feeling as he ever showed. So he was probably ready to go meet her in whatever place it is that spirits go after this.

And so he's made that journey, and the only time I'll see him again in this world is when I look in the mirror and see the family resemblance again; there's something in this face that feels like mine but borrows heavily from his.

I'm not sure I know exactly how to say what it is I want to say. But I feel like if he was here, he'd know what I meant.

Be kind

"In a world where you can be anything, be kind."

I still remember my brain exploding when I first saw a T-shirt with that slogan on it. Such a simple statement and so brimming with meaning.

The words resonate with those of us fortunate enough to have had mothers who said, "You can be anything you set out to be." And it's true: Whatever the world throws at you, you can overcome and reach your goals with persistence and hard work.

But if you set out to be kind, you open up a whole 'nother set of possibilities.

Imagine a world where kindness is a virtue. Of course we're already in that world, theoretically, but in practice the kind are constantly in danger of being steamrolled. The victory goes to the one who seeks it at all costs, the king of the mountain who races over everyone in his way and dies with the most toys.

What if the victory goes to the one who lends a hand, the one who seeks to lift all boats, the one who cares as much about how he wins as he does about winning itself?

What does it profit a go-getter if they gain the world but lose their soul?

In a world where you can be anything, be kind.

December: The darkest, brightest month

As someone who lives near a city famously associated with the phrase "frozen tundra," I must confess that I am not a fan of winter, and cold December brings the beginning of winter, so it might seem like a hard sell.

Among other things, however, December is the month when my parents were married, so deep into World War II that my dad's military rank was part of their wedding announcement, and 11 days later was my mom's 21st birthday. So the month has my roots going for it.

And then there's the joyful season of giving that reaches its zenith days after the winter solstice, and the month ends with a season of hope and new beginnings and resolutions to create something better out of all this.

And so, on balance, I tend to think of December more as the time of lingering autumn than as the arrival of unwelcome winter. Just don't get me started on January or February, just yet.

December is when we roll out a certain complement of songs that aren't sung during the other 11 months, songs of joy to the world, and the innocence of a newborn baby, and peace on Earth, and goodwill toward men, and why aren't those themes worth singing about all year long?

We tell the stories again — not just the story of the baby in the manger, but the story of a miser learning how to give, of a practical little girl discovering the power of believing in a magical jolly old elf, of a sad man discovering that he had been living a wonderful life all along, of a little boy with a sweet mom and a crusty but kind-hearted dad who wins a major award? Again, they are stories worth telling all year long.

December is the end of the cycle we measure by calendar and the month that brings the darkest day of the year, the day with the fewest hours of daylight, but a few days after the winter solstice our singing of songs and telling of stories reaches its climax, and we celebrate hope, in peace and with love.

And as the month ends, the days start growing longer again, a few minutes at a time. Even though we know it will get colder, we also know it will get brighter. We set our sights on a new year with a spirit of new resolve and a fresh slate. December is the coda of another magnificent symphony, and even if it wasn't the sweetest music we ever heard, the first notes of a new overture are waiting at the end of that final night.

Love Him out loud

I n December 2001 I had never heard of blogs or podcasts, but I did have a weekly column in the Green Bay News-Chronicle, as fine a newspaper as I've ever known, God rest its soul. This is a somewhat expanded version of what I submitted for Dec. 18, 2001, a week before Christmas.

- - - - -

As dreams go, this one was pretty vivid, not for any of the imagery but the intensity of the emotion. I can't remember the specific details, except for four words.

I dreamed a little traveling drama group had just finished performing a piece that was full of joy and finding meaning in life.

Someone asked the actors why they were so joyous, and they began to talk, quietly and almost apologetically, about Jesus Christ, looking furtively back and forth as if afraid to be discovered talking about the subject in public.

"Wait a minute," I said, and this is when the emotion welled up. "Why are you acting like you're ashamed that Jesus has made such an important difference in your life? There's no need to hide the fact. If you love Jesus, love Him out loud."

I awoke from the dream with those words literally echoing in my ears: Love Him out loud.

The funny thing about the dream was my role in it. I had no business saying anything like that or chastising people who hide their faith under the proverbial bushel basket. If anyone needed to hear that message, it was me.

I am not someone who wears his faith on his sleeve. Unless someone asks me, or if I let slip that I'm excited to hear about a Christian musician who is playing a concert somewhere nearby, the source of whatever joy, peace or optimism I convey usually remains unspoken.

It's a shame that we have developed this societal attitude that it's not polite to mention or celebrate God in civil conversation. Something of the richness and freedom of America is lost when we allow ourselves to be intimidated by people who claim to be offended or belittled by public displays of faith in God.

I enjoy learning about the different ways that we have to get us in touch with the Creator.

I love that the Oneida Nation built its public school in the shape of a turtle, illustrating its tradition that the Creator built the world on the back of a huge turtle. I wish we would celebrate the rich melting pot culture of America by inviting all religious traditions into our schools, not shutting them all out.

I have never been offended, and I do not feel belittled, when Catholics finish the Lord's prayer before what I as a Protestant have always been taught was the last line: "For thine is the kingdom ..."

I do not feel threatened to know that others believe Jesus was a great teacher but not the Messiah, or even that He did not or does not exist at all.

All I know is an overwhelming feeling of gratitude about the birth that we Christians have come to celebrate every Dec. 25, and the death and resurrection that we recall every spring. My journey of faith brought me to a personal relationship with a living Jesus.

The important thing, I think, is that we believe in something bigger than ourselves. That search defines who we are as individuals and as a people, and I pray that what you have found along your journey fills you with as much love and peace as the Christ has brought to me. If not, check Him out. If so, love Him out loud.

A spirit of love does not have room for hatred of other faiths, other traditions. Such a simple concept, taught by almost all faiths, and yet so often tossed aside: Love one another.

Don't be afraid, in a spirit of love and respect for others, to say what has made a difference in your life: Love Him out loud.

He doth not sleep

"The fruit of the spirit is love, joy, peace, kindness, goodness, faithfulness, gentleness and self-control." We are tempted to hang our heads like Longfellow and say, "There is no ..."

But, like Longfellow, when we lift our heads back up, we are likely to discover "God is not dead, nor doth He sleep; The Wrong shall fail, the Right prevail, with peace on earth, good-will to men."

It's everywhere we turn, in the smile of child watching a puppy scamper across a yard, in the hug of a friend in an hour of need, in the laughter of an old man with a long-lost friend, in the tears of strangers leaving a sentimental movie together, in the strains of a street musician's lonely song, in the rustle of birds taking flight all at once, in the murmur of young lovers with their foreheads touching, and a hundred other sights and sounds every moment, every hour, every day.

This appears to be a harsh and divided world until we lift our eyes to meet our neighbors' and see the common ground on which we stand — the hope for a better tomorrow, the willingness to live and let live, the fruit of the spirit.

This is a grand and glorious world inhabited by grand and

glorious people and surrounded by so much that is grand and glorious.

Of course, many people spend their time with fingers pointed at much that is wrong with what they see, missing the many bits of evidence that The Wrong will fail and The Right prevail. It's almost as if they have a vested interest in The Wrong. I'm not here, however, to question their motives.

I'm simply pointing out the obvious: The fruit of the spirit is in evidence everywhere we turn, if we will simply look and see.

The future perfect tense

The night's entertainment was *The Life List*, a sweet movie based on a novel by Lori Nelson Spielman. I enjoyed the movie so much I just added Spielman's book to my phone as my latest Audible acquisition. The movie (and I presume the book) is about a young woman whose life has not proceeded the way her 13-year-old self envisioned when she compiled the list of things she intended to do in her lifetime.

I wonder what my 13-year-old self might say about how it has turned out.

I wonder what my 72-year-old self would say. Bless the broken road that led me straight to this place? Perhaps. I did so many silly and/or stupid things along the way, but today wouldn't have happened without all those twists and turns. I wanted to be a reporter, an author, a singer-songwriter, a disc jockey, and it all came true, just without the fame and financial independence and all that.

Wait. It's too early for summing things up. The journey is still ongoing, and who knows how many more stops are on the way?

I wanted to be Ray Bradbury when I grew up, or Paul Harvey, or Lester Dent, or E.E. Cummings, but of course I was Warren P. Bluhm all along, incorporating snippets of the poetic storyteller and the radio commentator and the pulp novelist and the flaunter of convention into whatever this is that I am.

And let's be clear: Early in that last run-on sentence, I said "I was," but the last two words — the latest words — were "I am."

It's too early to put me in the past tense, and let me encourage you, too, dear reader. You and I may not have turned out the way we envisioned our lives way back when, and maybe there've been some painful endings that made us want to quit, but we have a pulse and we're breathing, so the story is not over.

There are stories yet to be told, and adventures yet to be embarked upon. Stop looking back — look around — and keep moving forward. Who told you the best years are behind you? There's still a future to live, and it's just as possible the best is yet to be. You don't know what the future will bring until you step into it.

How many gardens

Not long ago I reached the 1,700th consecutive day that I have posted on my blog since first I decided to try posting daily for three months. August through October, 2020, amounted to the first 92 days. I decided to keep going on Day 93, and the momentum continues to carry the streak along.

What an amazing and often trying 1,700 days it has been. When I started the streak on August. 1, 2020, we were living in Bizarro World, forced to stay at home, isolated from one another. The world got even stranger as I wrote and tried to make sense of it all. Some of my thoughts coalesced into a creed of sorts.

"Love your neighbor, and all of us are neighbors." That's not precisely a creed, it's a command, one that comes from the real ruler, whom I love, also as commanded.

Politics is not the center of our lives, although it's easy to fall into the trap of thinking that it is. To the extent that a politician is pursuing liberty and peace among humanity, s/he has my attention. The vast majority of politicians are enemies of liberty and peace, alas.

"I don't know how many gardens I have left," my beloved Red would say as she worked the soil every spring and summer, and she had fewer gardens left than we realized or could have imagined. It makes no sense to sow seeds of discord and despair when we have an unknown amount of time left to sow seeds of peace and harmony and understanding. There is joy to be found and happiness to discover, and that is how I want my last gardens to grow.

I could have 24 more years to make gardens while I live to see my 96th birthday in 2049, should I live as long as my father did — or this could be my final entry before something unforeseen occurs later today. In either case, or in any case, let my efforts from here be in the name of love.

I have no quarrel with my neighbors. I mourn, but I am comforted. Let me be small and meek. Let me be a peacemaker, let me be merciful, let me seek to be pure in heart. That is the garden I want to sow; that is the garden we all need to sow.

About the author

Thank you for reading this book. I grew up in New Jersey but became a native Wisconsinite sometime during the four years I attended Ripon College. I have now lived in the Badger State three times as long as I lived in the Garden State. I have loved and lost and loved again, and as of this writing, I live not far from the shores of the bay of Green Bay with two adorable golden retrievers, Dejah and Summer.

I have now published 10 collections of blog posts and the sixth since I began blogging every day in 2020. Hard to believe but I've been blogging for two decades now, ever since not long after I found out what a blog is.

Let me tell you a little bit about these 10 books. Of course, I do this in part to encourage you to purchase one or more of the other nine, but also to share just a little bit more of me.

1. *Refuse to be Afraid* (2010). Not long after I started blogging, I found myself returning to this theme. The world is inhabited by fear mongers who purport to be protective leaders but, by their actions, reveal themselves to be rather power hungry control freaks. H.L. Mencken said it best: "The whole aim of practical politics is to keep the populace alarmed (and hence clamorous to be led to safety) by

menacing it with an endless series of hobgoblins, most of them imaginary." This first collection encourages the reader to resist the fear, free yourself and follow your dreams.

2. *A Scream of Consciousness* (2011) arose from my introduction to *The Sacrament of the Present Moment*, a centuries-old collection of sermons by Father Jean-Pierre de Caussade. Its premise: There has to be something more to life than moving through a haze. And every now and then, it gets to you. You just want to wake up, smile at God and the universe and shout: "I'm alive! I'm here! I'm ready to make a difference!" That's a scream of consciousness. This book is about getting conscious and staying alive, moment by moment.

3. *A Bridge at Crossroads* (2019) is subtitled *101 Encouragements*, and that's what the book is. Not long after being removed from my dream job, I took a walk through a preserve called Crossroads at Big Creek, and sitting on a bench near a bridge over the creek, I began to write: "When you are sad – for there will come a time when you are sad – remember a time you were so happy you wished this moment would last forever – because it does last forever as long as you remember ..." That became the opening line in the first of the 101 encouragements.

4. I wrote a poem called *How to Play a Blue Guitar* that became the title piece in a collection of essays, short stories and poems. One morning in April 2020, I reviewed the 24 entries I had collected so far and discovered that they seemed to hold together as a unit. Before I could second-guess myself, and using the miracle of modern technology, I published the book by the end of the day. This, by the way, is where you may find "Wildflower Man," my most well-known short story.

5. In the middle of the darkness that was the COVID-19 lock-downs, I felt a need to celebrate lightness and so published *Gladness is Infectious* (released Dec. 31, 2020), a book of celebrations. Each of us has two choices every day: Add to the beauty or add to the despair. The choice is there, every morning – to ride the light out of

darkness and live in peace, striving for harmony against the discord. This little book was my humble blow against the dark.

6. *Full: Rockets, Bells & Poetry* (2021) is a collection of notes, aphorisms and poems, really three much shorter books in one volume: "The Creative Soul," reflections on making art and the power of words; "Live Free Or Die," thoughts about liberty, self-expression and emerging from dystopia; and "You Can Do This," encouraging words of finding light in a darkening world.

7. *Echoes of Freedom Past* (2022), subtitled *Reclaiming and Restoring Liberty*, is another response to the lockdowns. There is a section about freedom and the Bill of Rights. There is a section about what had been happening in the past several years, and how everything changed, almost in a blink. And there is a section of hope for the future, because most of us want to be free, want to be left alone to live our personal vision of our best life, and want to respect everyone's right to life, liberty, and pursuit of happiness, as long as they don't infringe on other people's equal rights to those things.

8. *It's Going to Be All Right* (2022) is another book of encouragements, this time on the theme of how despite that the world has gotten angrier and meaner and more afraid, if you reach inside to a calm place, you'll find the most basic of truths: It's going to be all right. Oh, change is inevitable, and tomorrow will not look like yesterday, but it's going to be all right.

9. *A Declaration of Peace* (2024) grew from the morning my beloved Red died, as I read passages from the Bible to her as she had requested. I saw that the last words I had spoken to her were from the gospel of Matthew: "'Love the Lord your God with all your heart and with all your soul and with all your mind.' This is the first and greatest commandment. And the second is like it: 'Love your neighbor as yourself.' All the Law and the Prophets hang on these two commandments." From that moment I began advocating a simple creed — Love your neighbor, and we are all neighbors — and for an end to humanity's declarations of war.

10. *See the World!* (2025) is about the need to stand still, look

around and pay attention. The world is full of wonders from the microscopic to the immense, and too often we let our eyes glaze over so that we miss what is right in front of us — a world so beautiful and packed with such amazing things. This book grew from my resolution to take time and see those wonders moment by moment.

www.ingramcontent.com/pod-product-compliance
Lightning Source LLC
Chambersburg PA
CBHW051258020426

42333CB00026B/3268